Peeping Lily And Her Friends Coloring Book

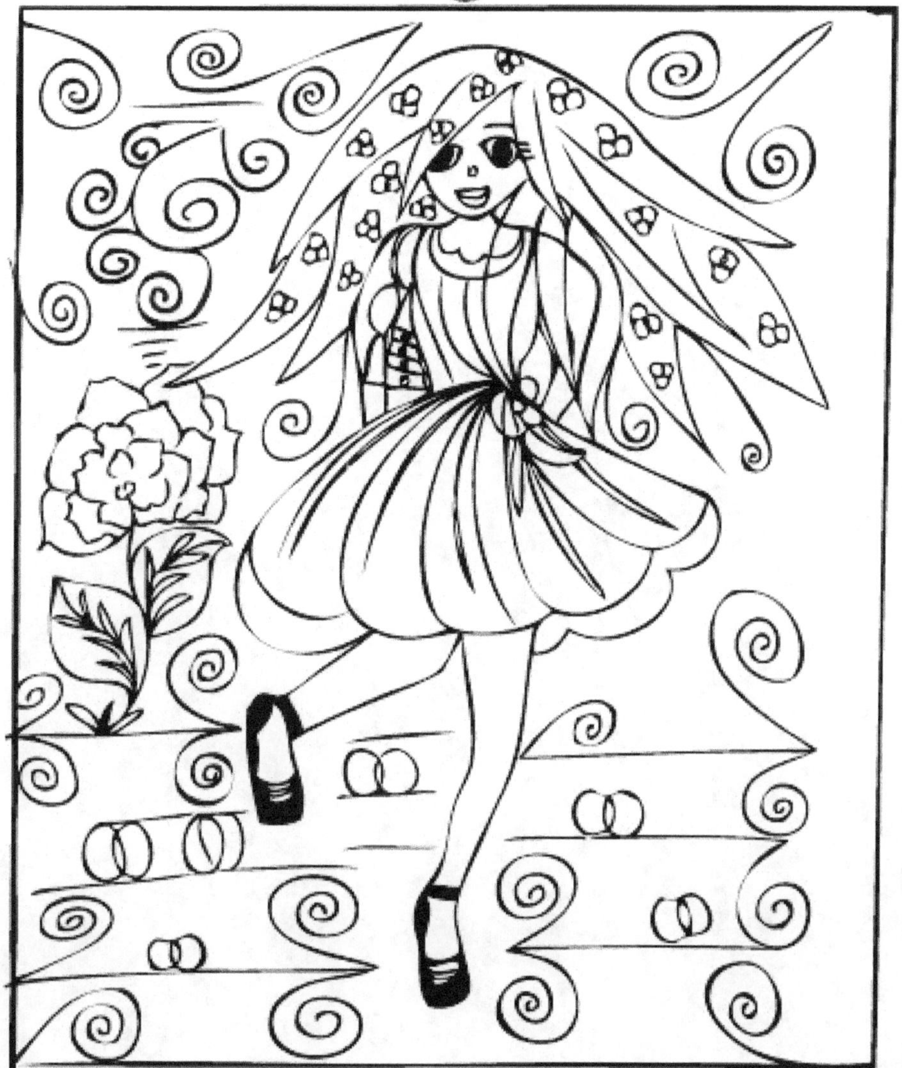

by Terry Urban

ISBN: 1515333590
ISBN-13: 978-1515333593

Cover art and artwork by Terry Urban

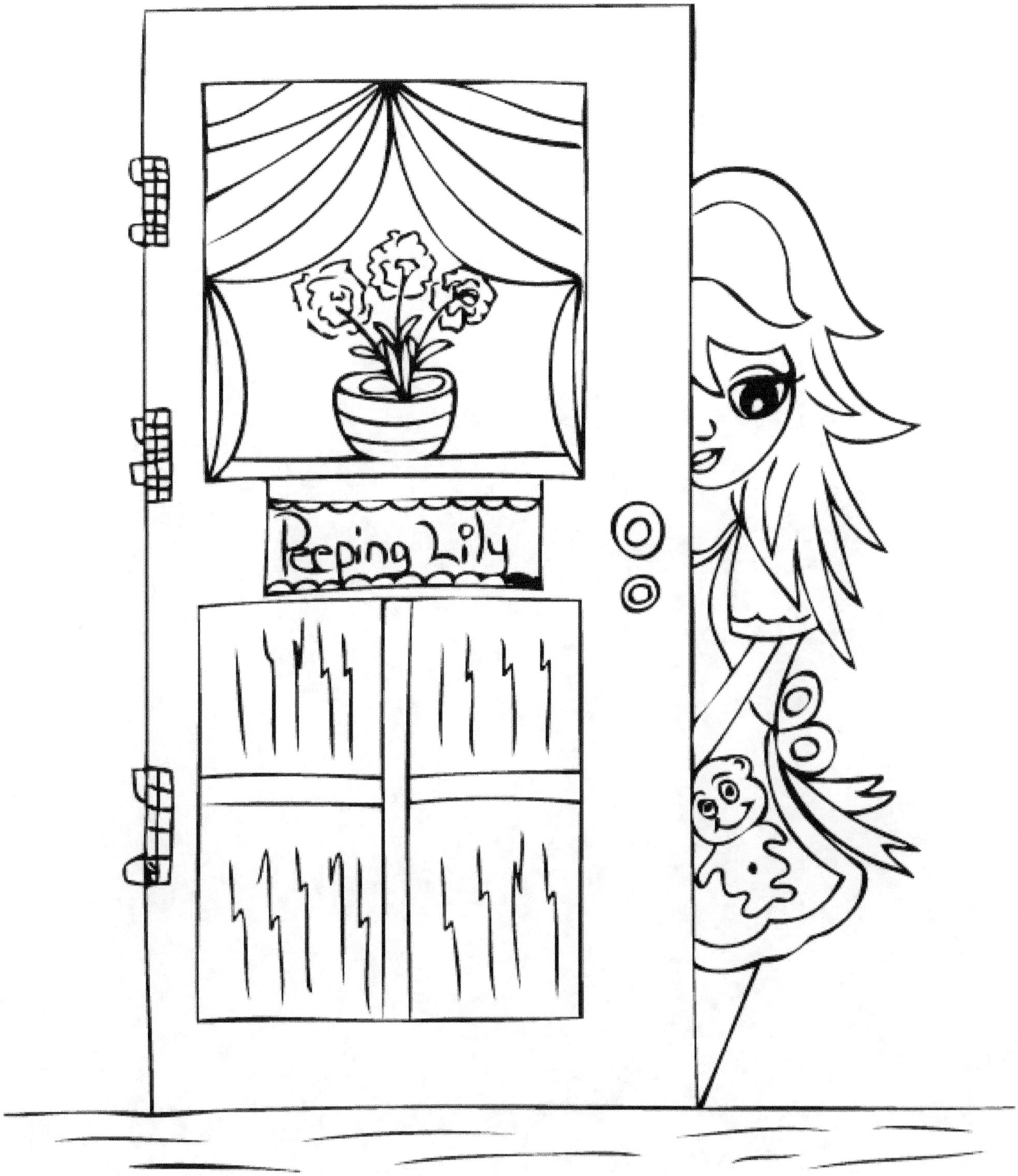
Peeping Lily

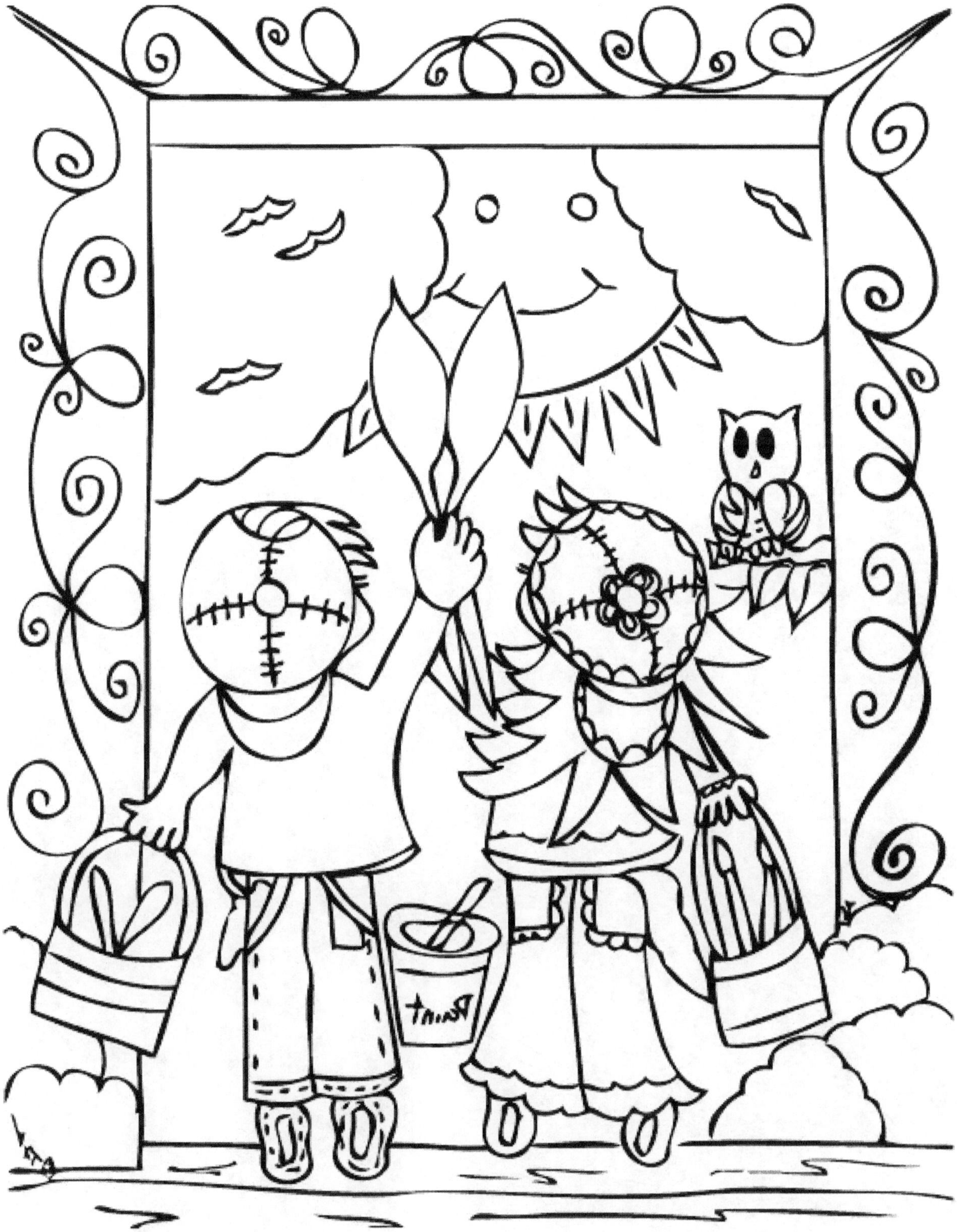
Paint

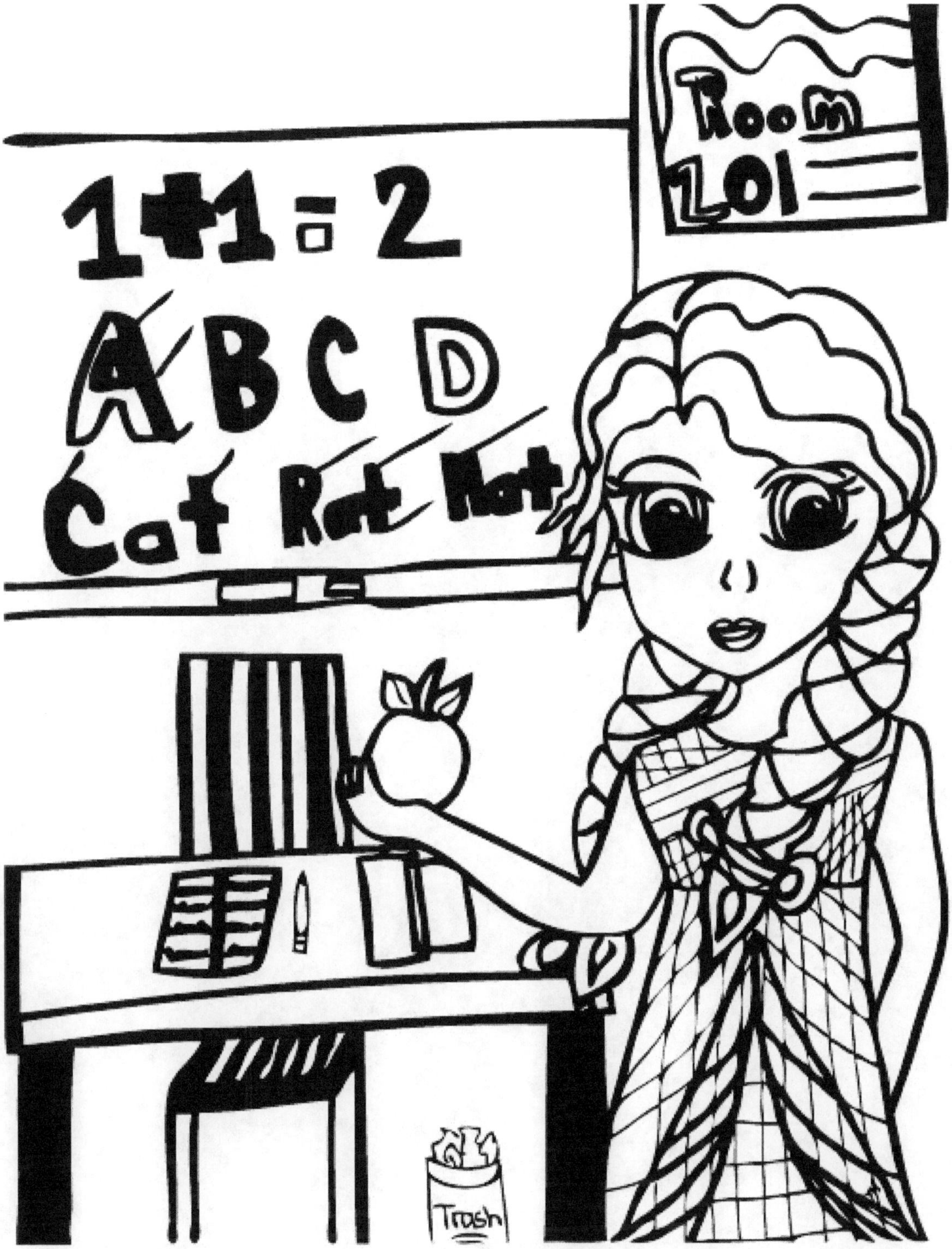
Room
201
1+1=2
ABCD
Cat Rat Hat
Trash

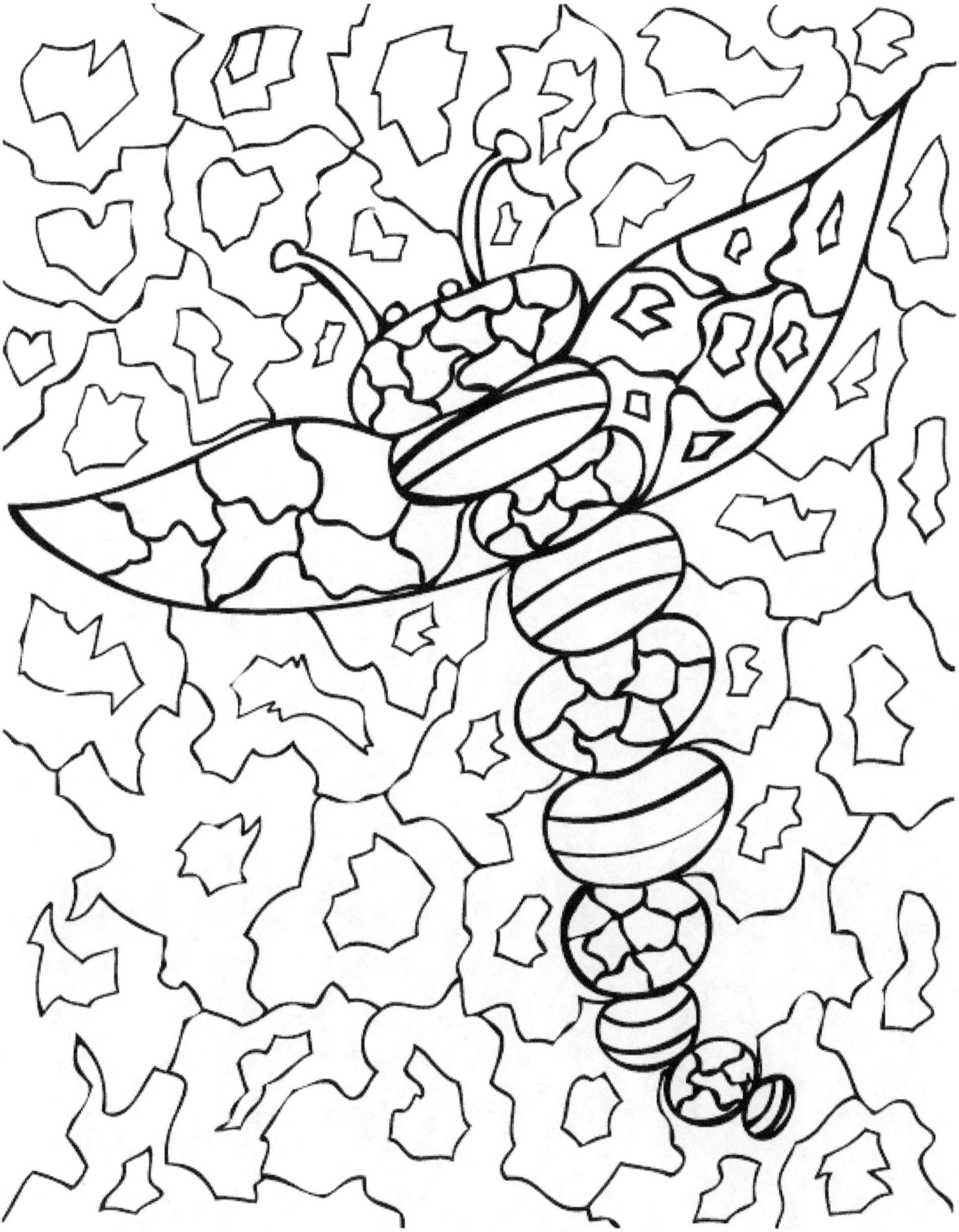

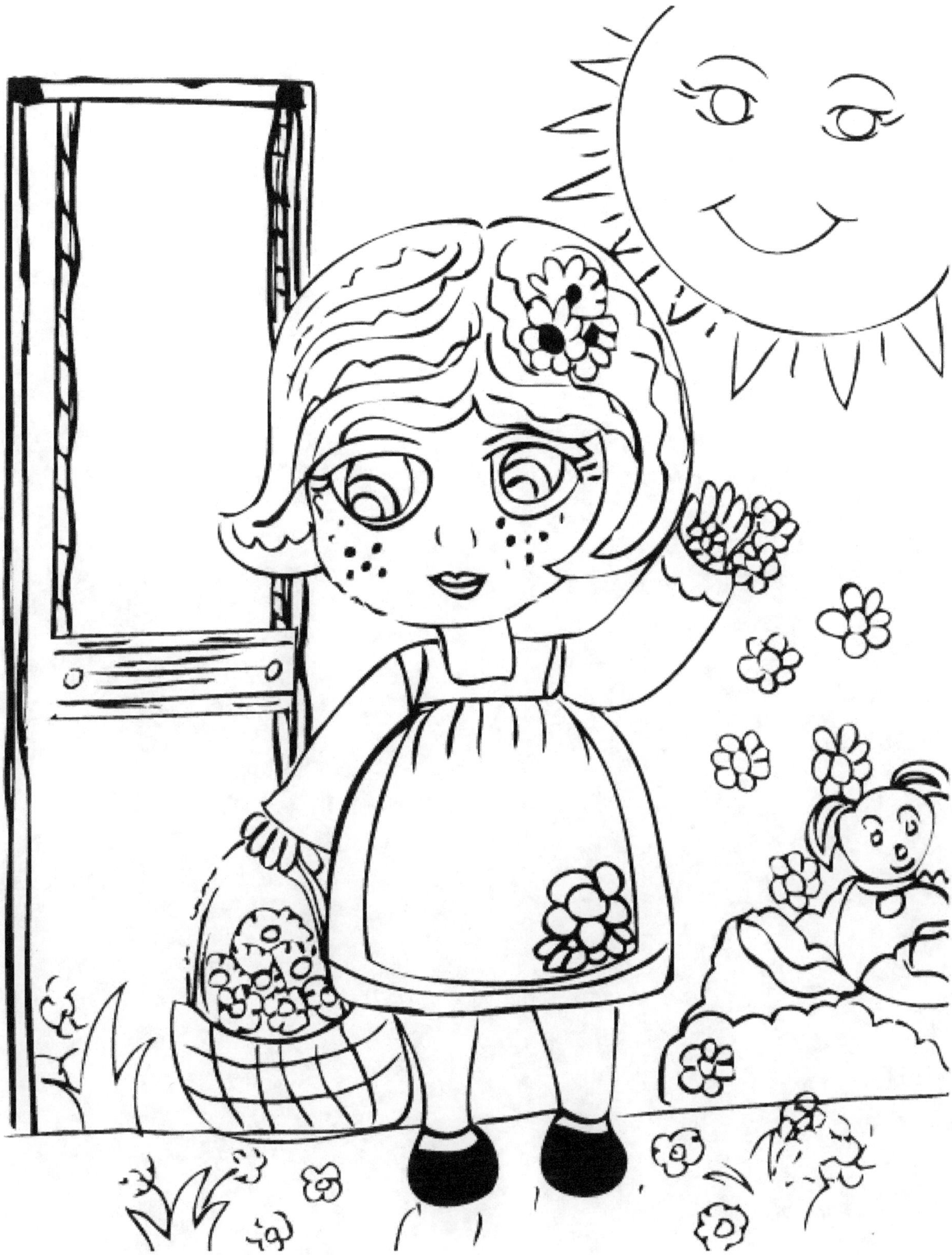

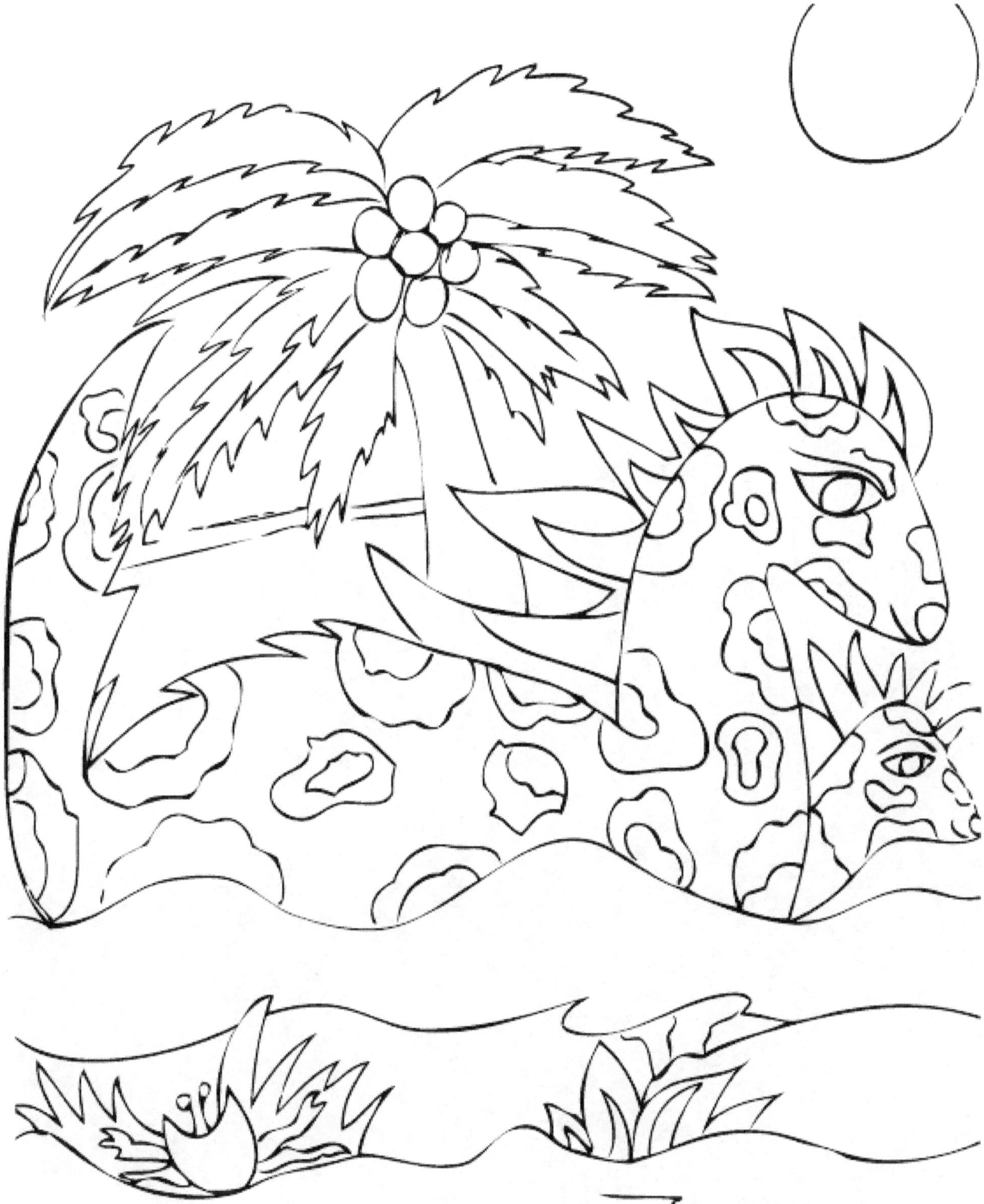

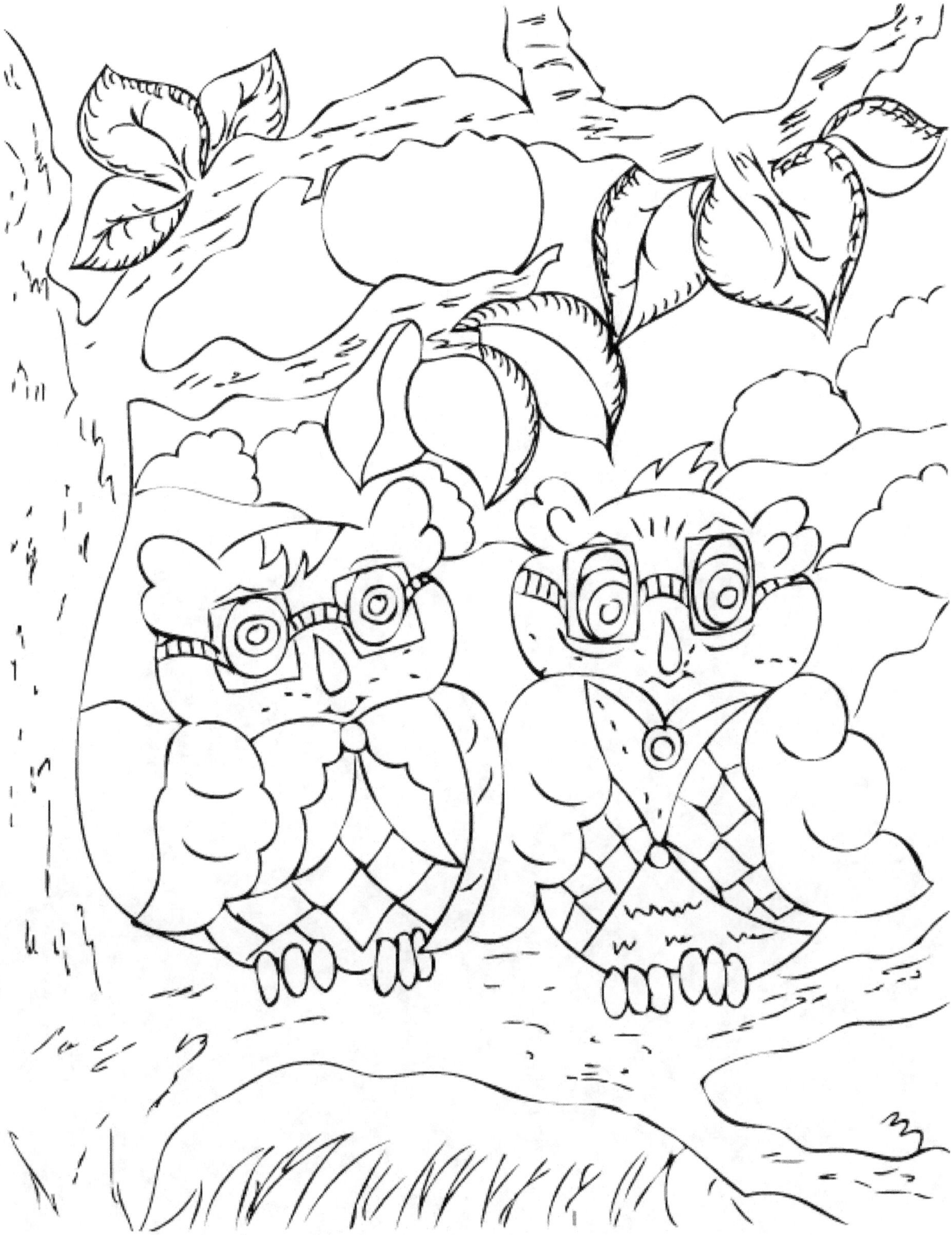

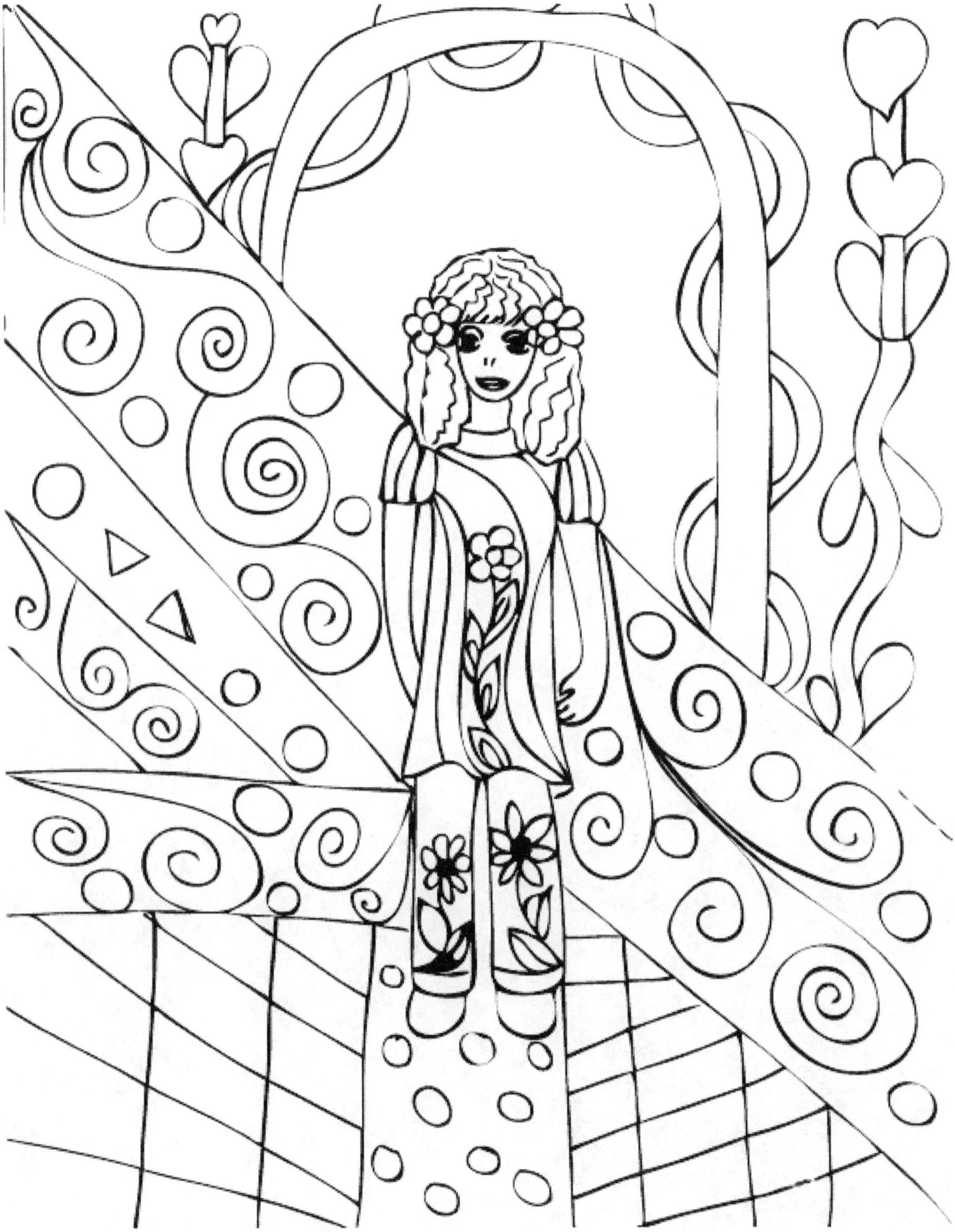

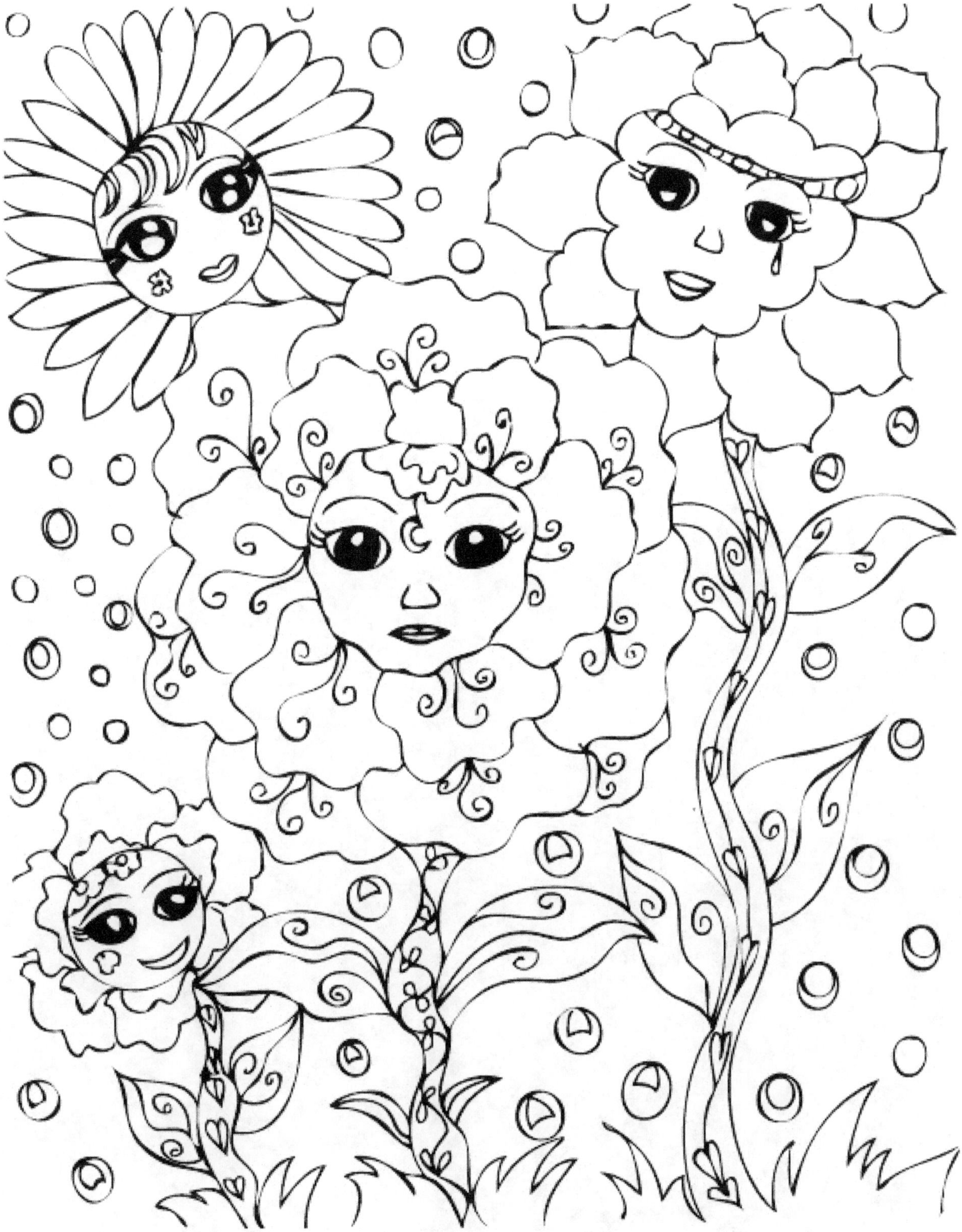

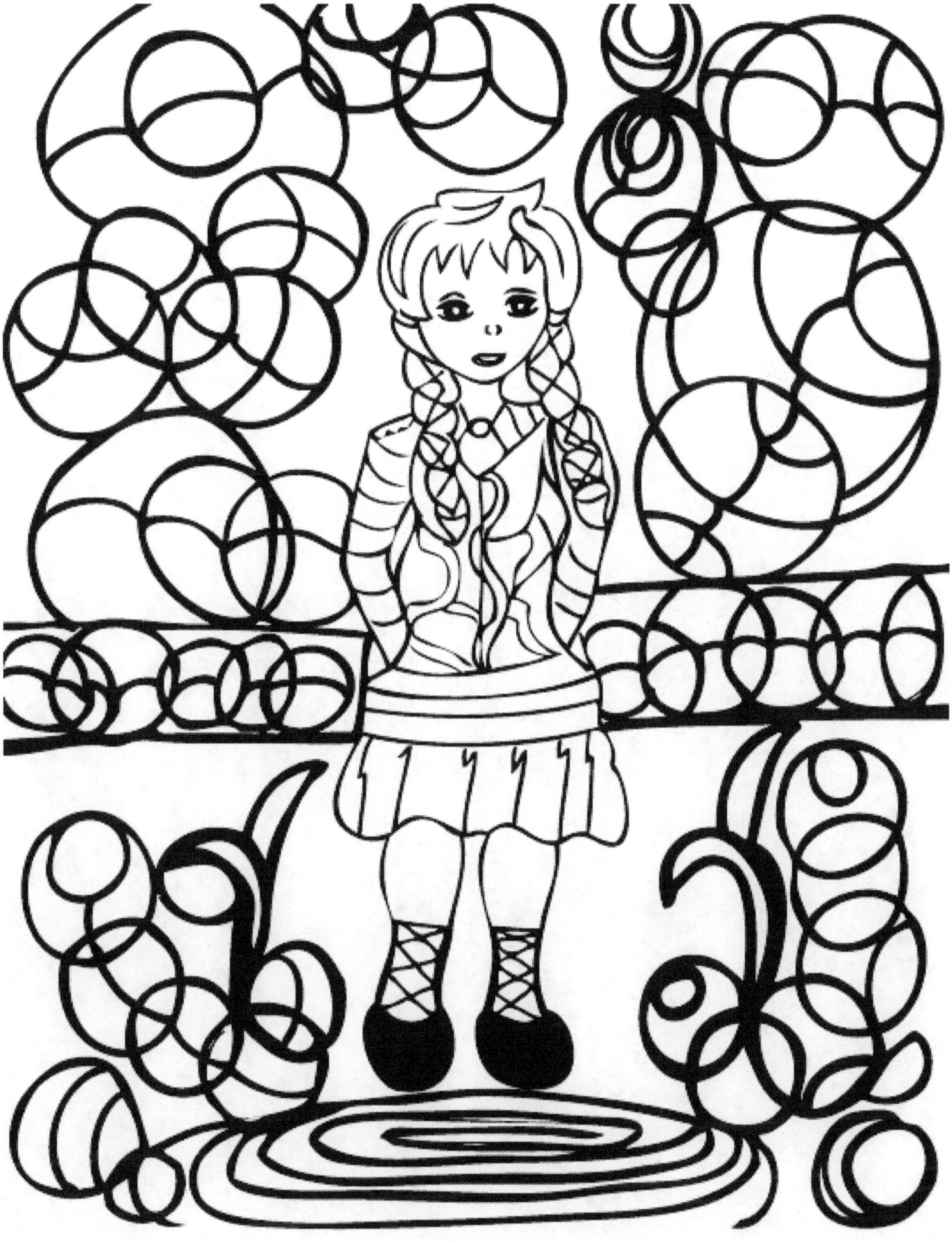

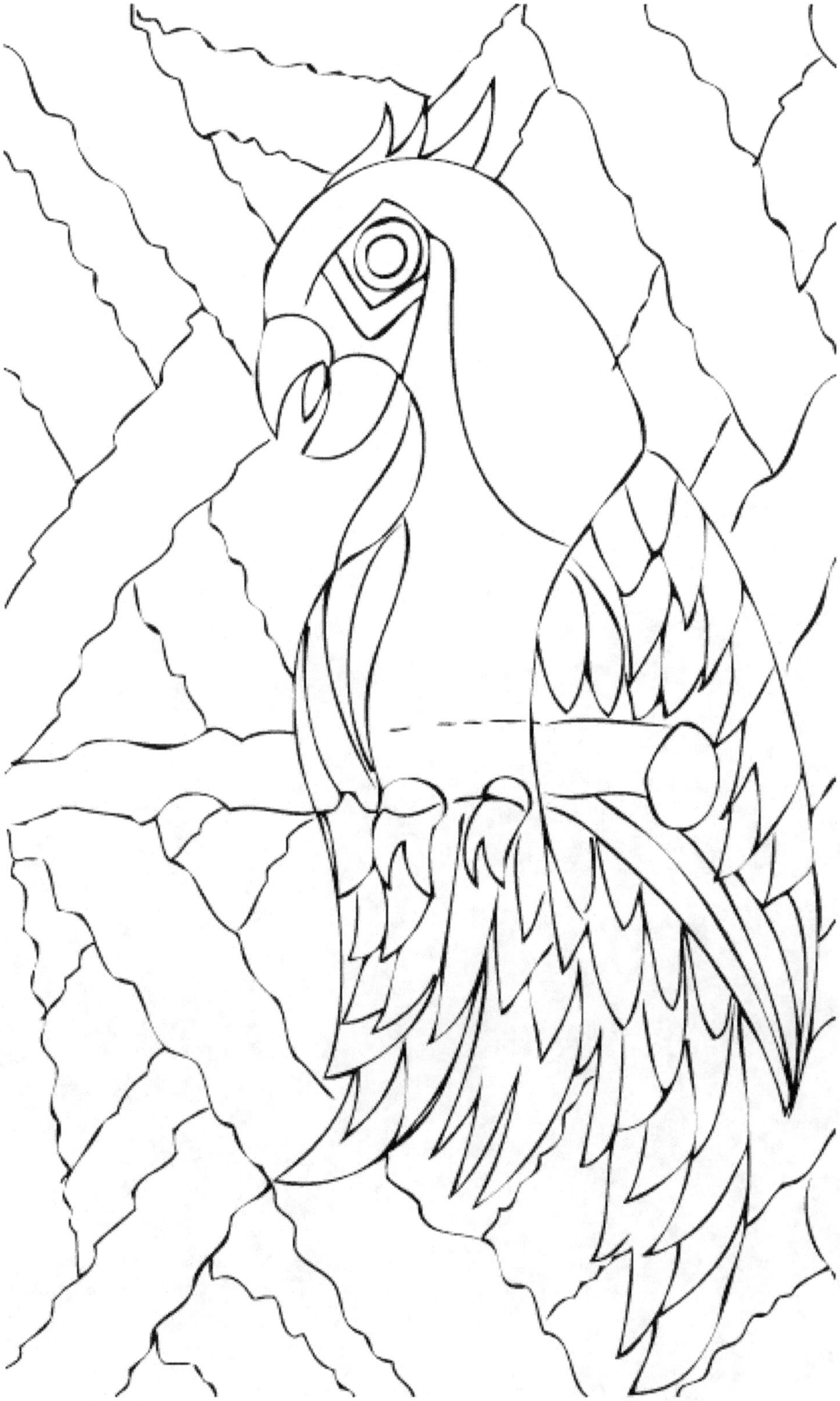

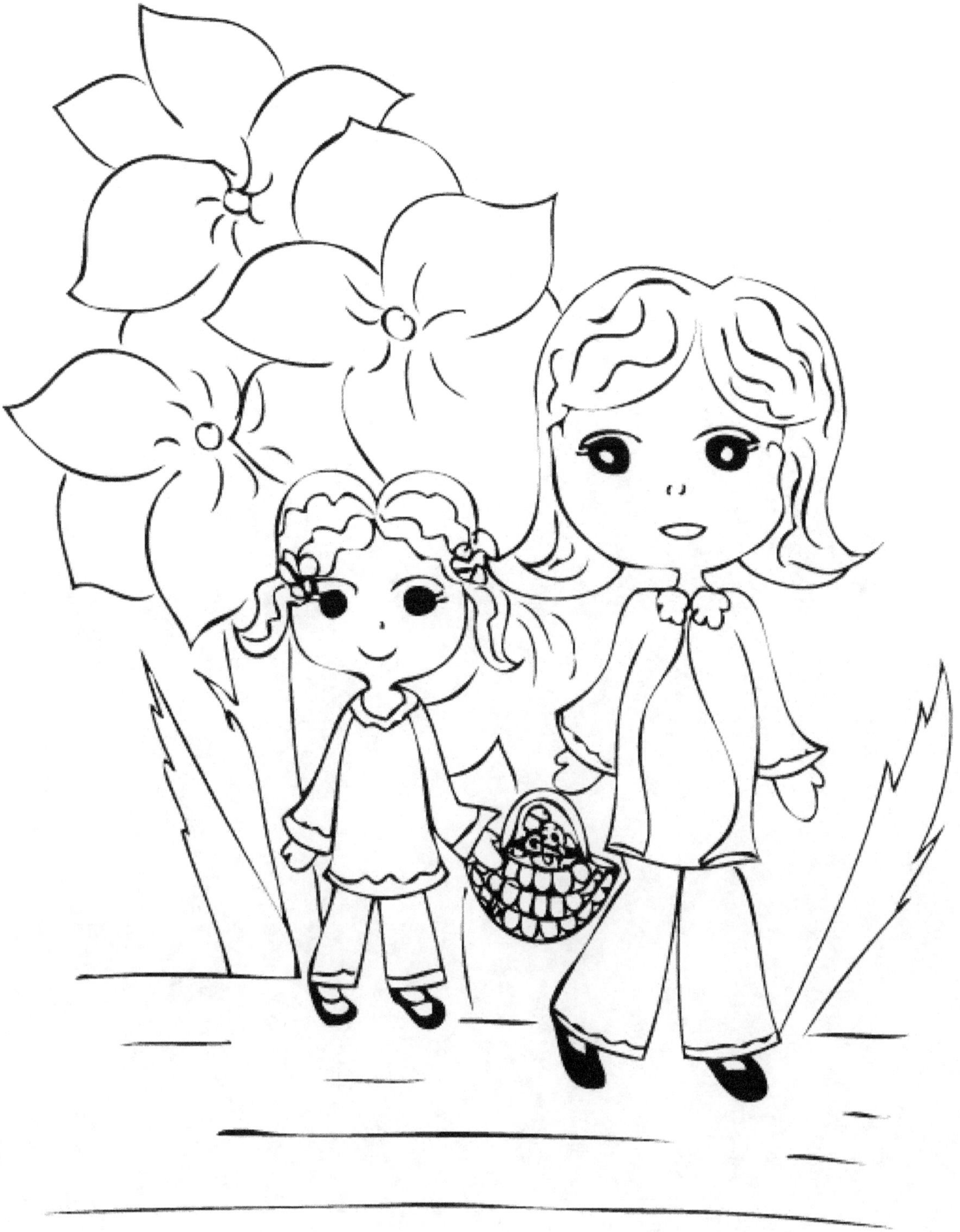

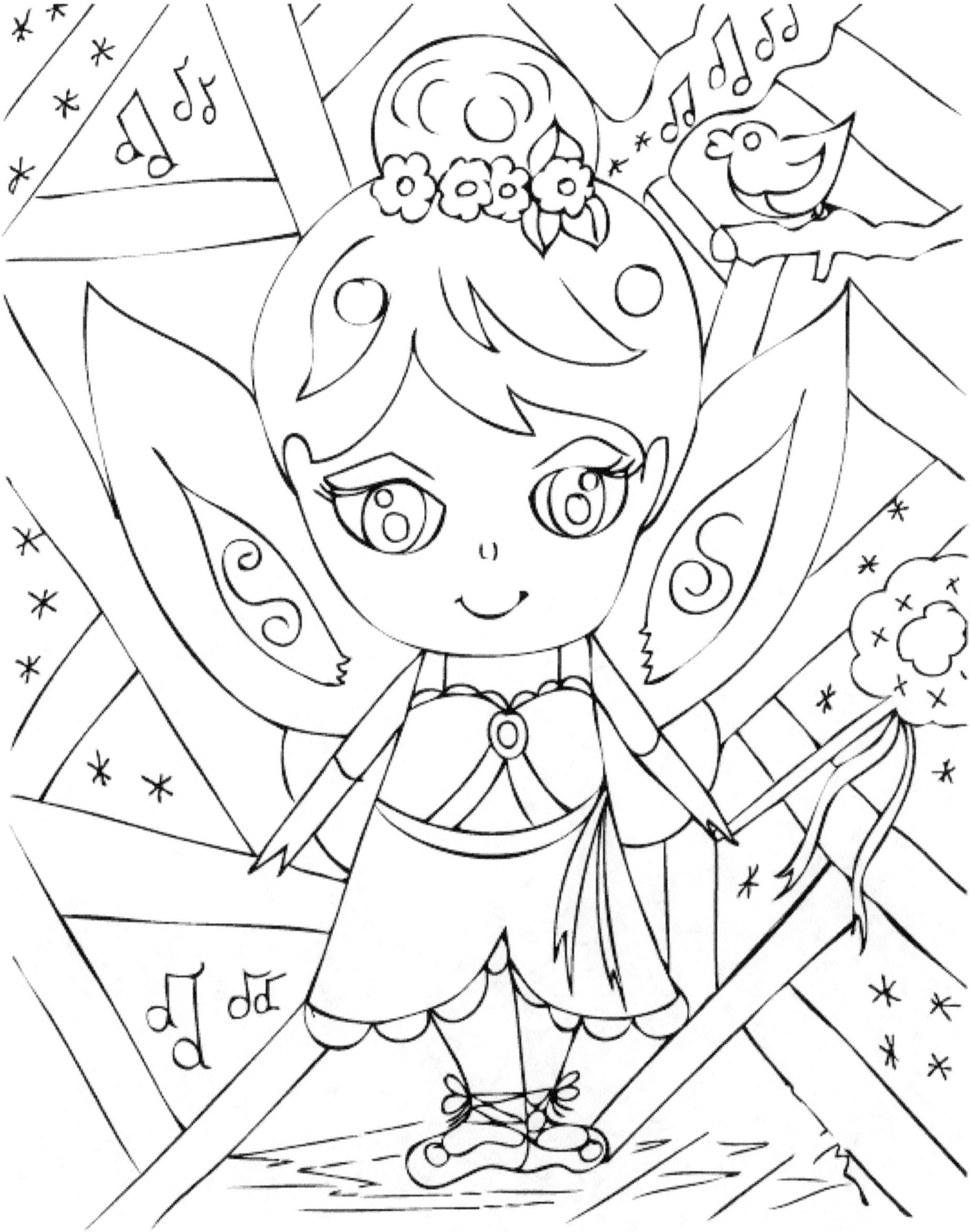

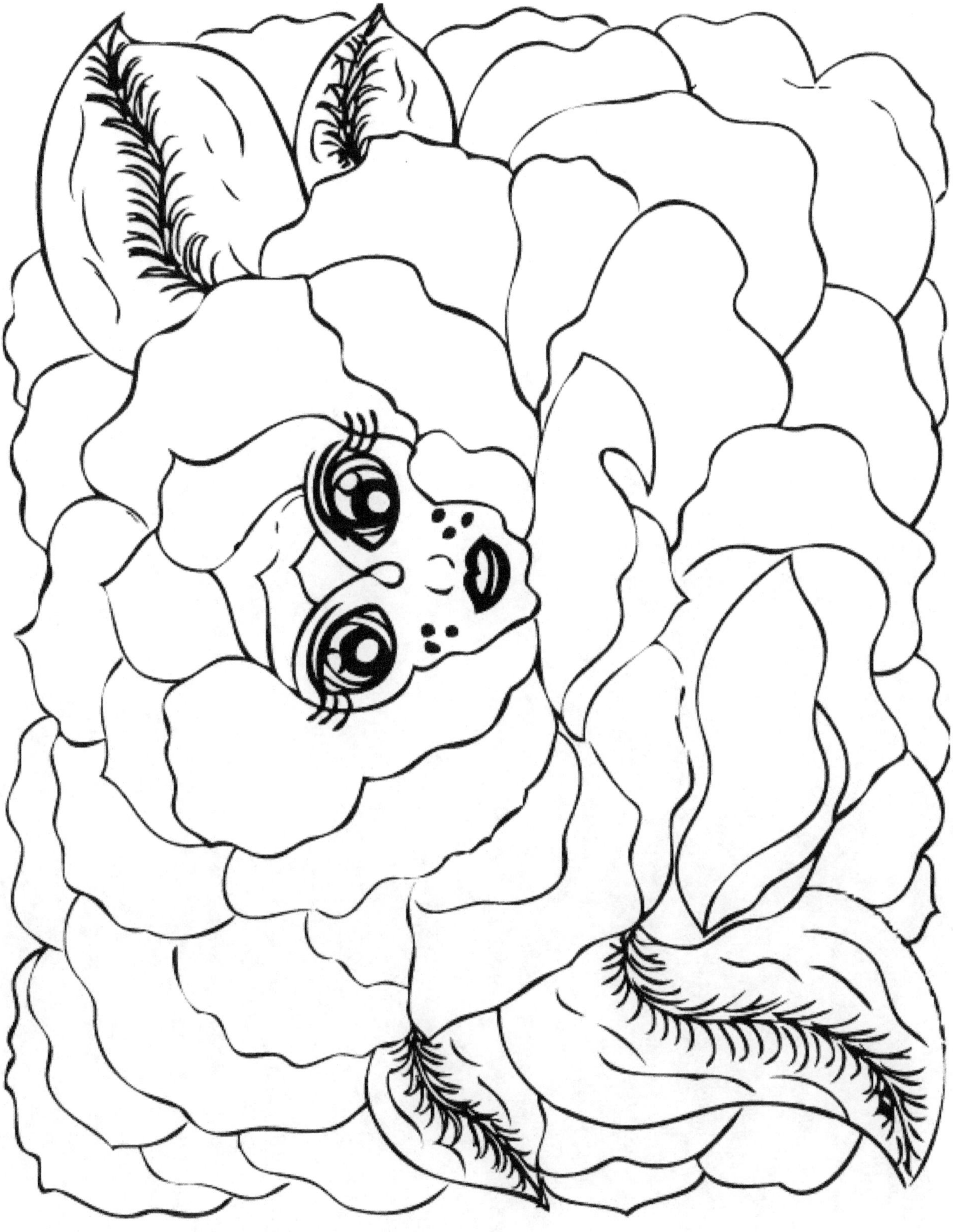

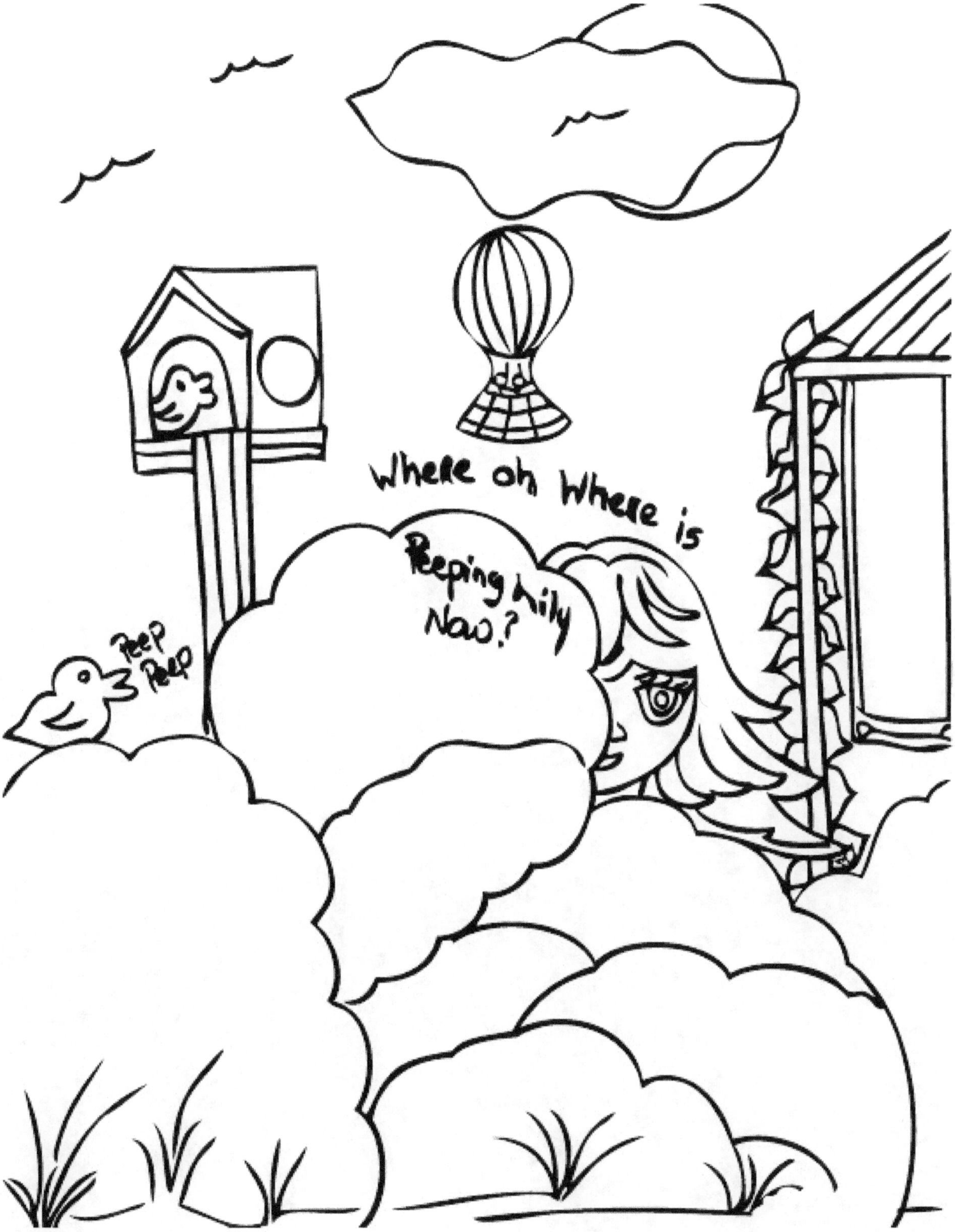
Where oh Where is
Peeping Lily
Now?
Peep
Peep

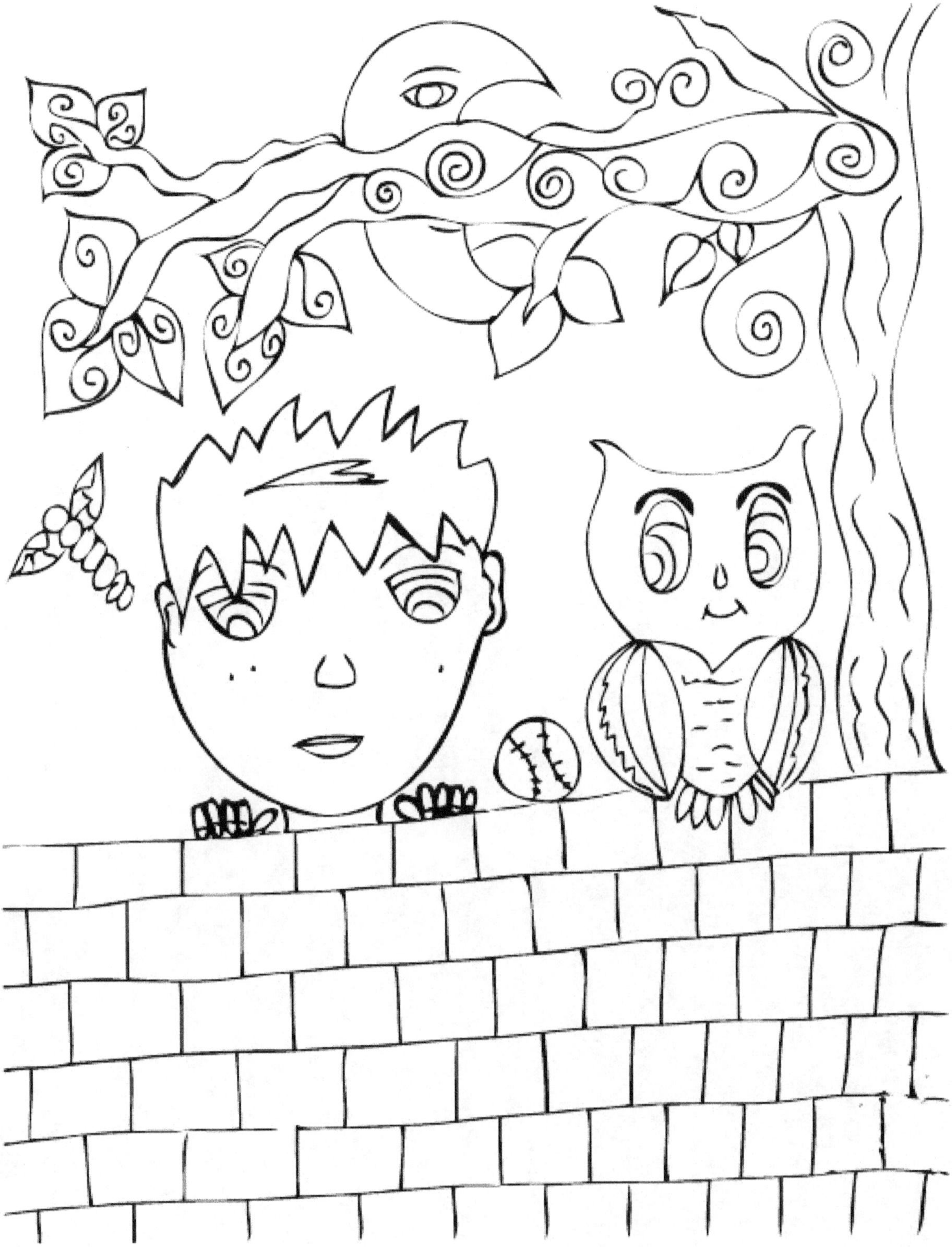

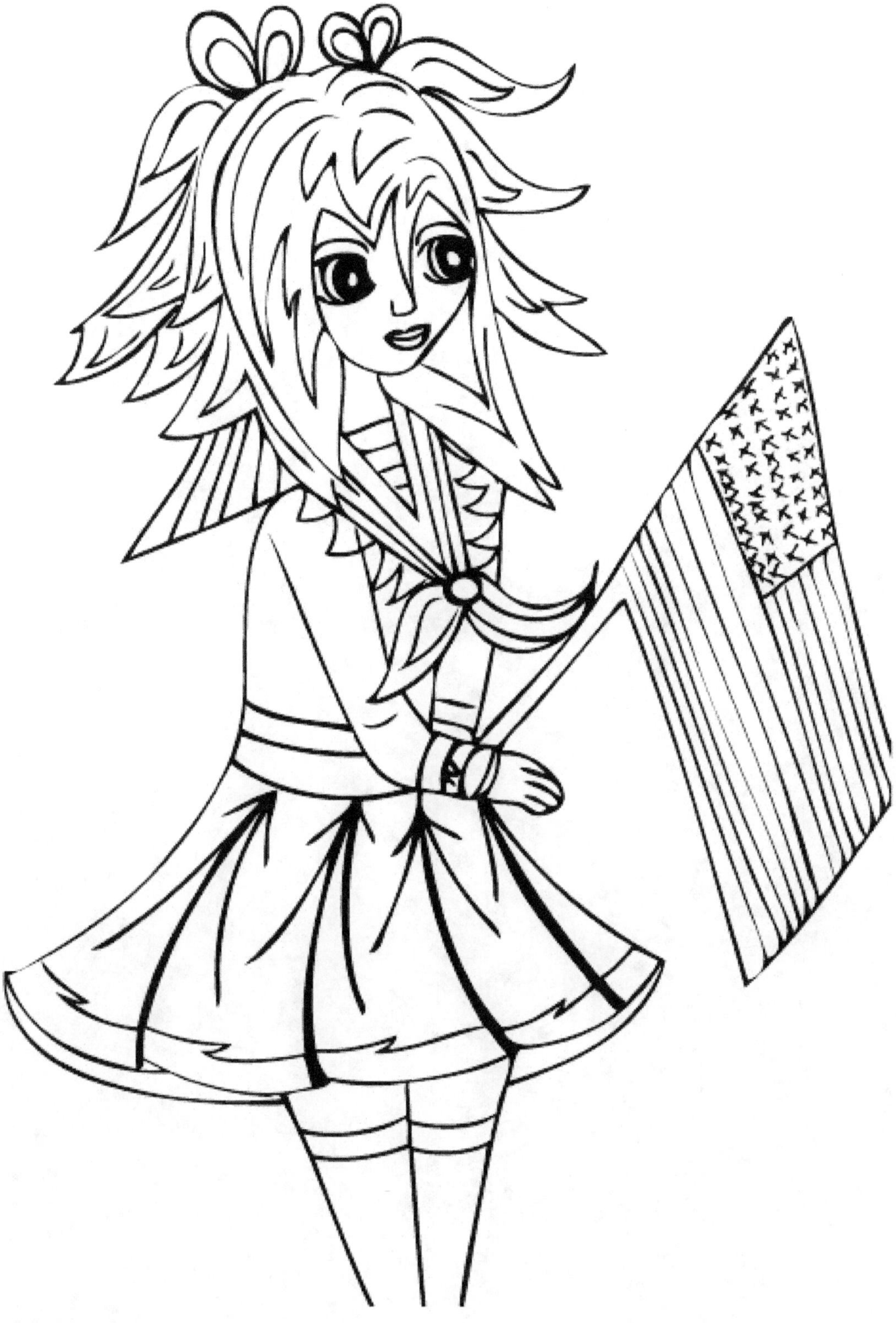

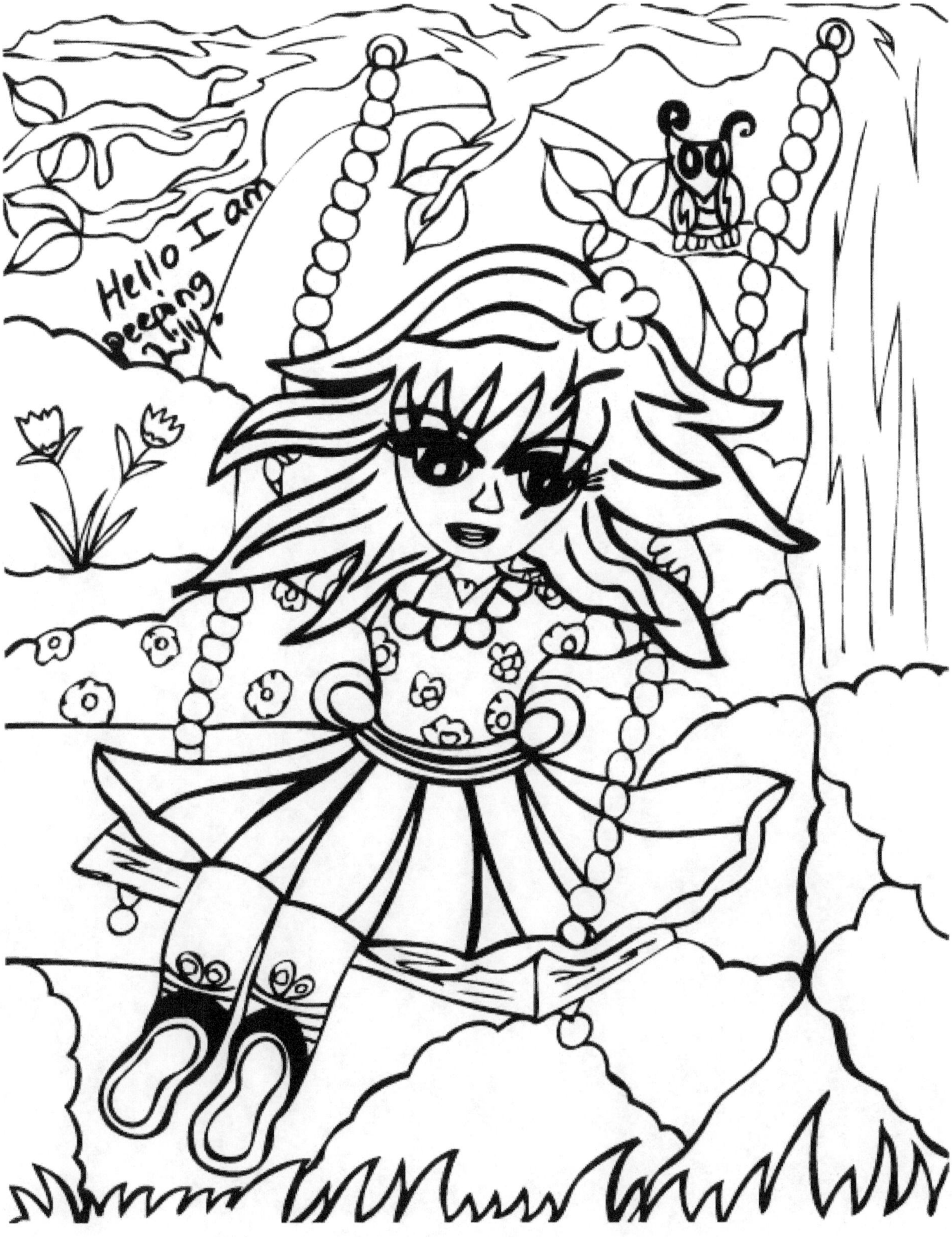
Hello I am
peeping Lily

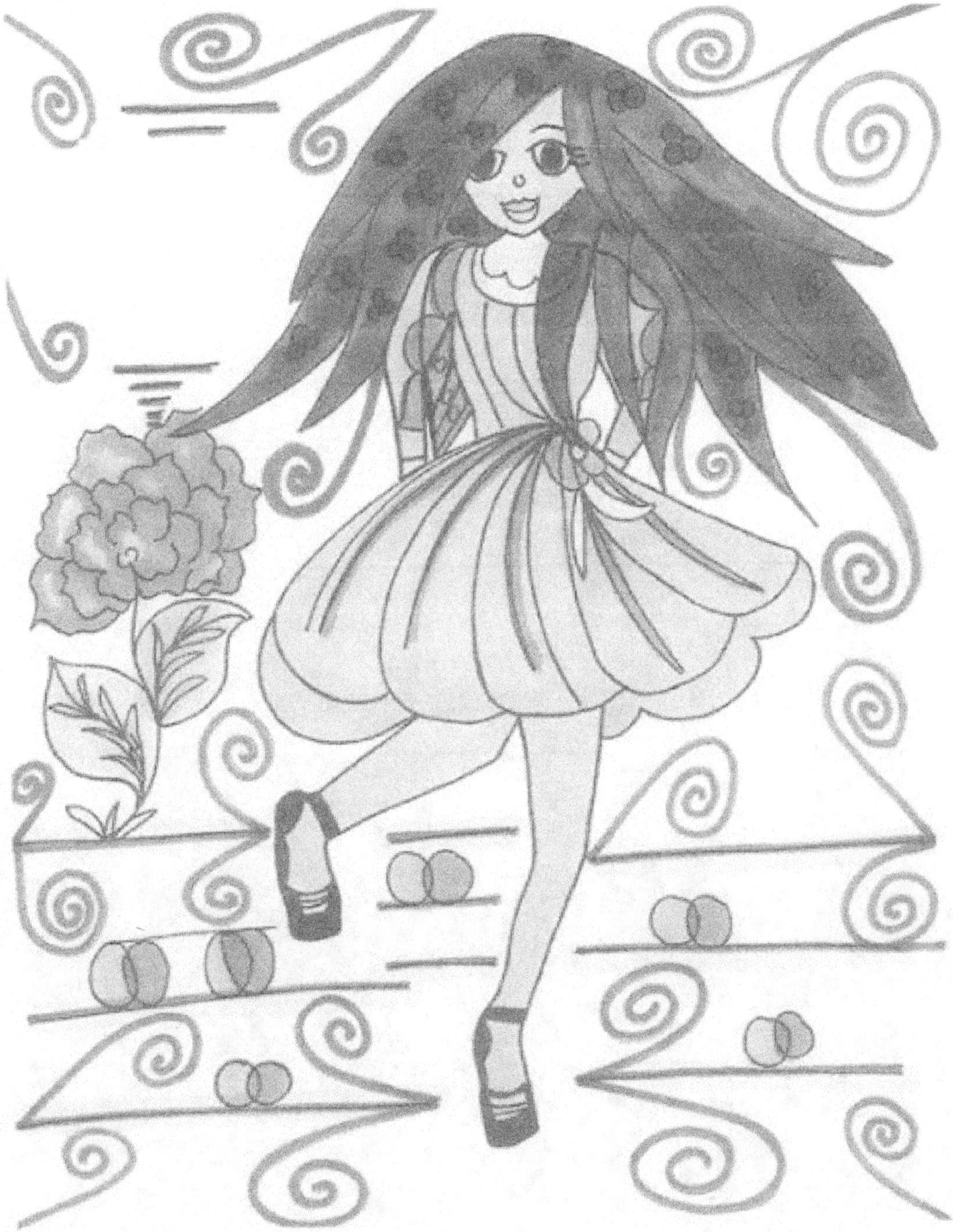

www.ingramcontent.com/pod-product-compliance
Lightning Source LLC
Chambersburg PA
CBHW080618180526
45168CB00007B/2961